PERFECT PEACE

SHAHINA QURESHI

Copyright © Shahina Qureshi
All Rights Reserved.

This book is dedicated to my parents, siblings, and close friends. They are the most meaningful people in my life; without them, I would not be as happy or prosperous as I am today. They've always been there for me when I needed them. I hope that by sharing my story with the world, they'll see how much their support means to me.

To my parents—I can't thank you enough for loving me unconditionally and teaching me to love myself the same way. To my siblings—you are my best friends and constant sources of encouragement. To those closest to me—thank you for always being there for me, even when I need it most.

Contents

Preface

I want to take a moment to thank everyone who helped me get this far, and all the people who will be reading it when it's done. I hope that you find this book as inspiring as I did when I first began writing it.

I'm so grateful for my family and friends, who were willing to be patient while I worked on this project (and even more patient when they realized how slow I was). To my beta readers: thank you so much for taking the time to read these words, even though they were sometimes challenging to interpret. Thank you also for telling me where you thought there were problems or holes in my story.

To my readers: thank you for taking the time to read this book! Please feel free to let me know what you think of it at any time—I'd love to hear from you!

Acknowledgements

Writing this book has been a journey that I never thought I would take. It was a challenge and one that I faced alone. But it was also an opportunity that I had to seize, and one that allowed me to grow as a person.

I would like to thank my parents for always encouraging me to do things that made me feel uncomfortable. They are the reason why I am who I am today. My siblings, who are so different from each other but so similar in their own ways, were equally instrumental in my success as an author. They helped me find my voice as an author and pushed me toward making this dream come true. I would also like to thank my special friend for making this story amazing, adventurous, and beautiful. I also like to thank my cousin and her son for the beautiful memories.

Lastly, I would like to thank you for reading this book. Your support has been instrumental in making this project a success for me. I hope that you will enjoy reading about it as much as I did writing it!

The Grand Mosque is a place of spirituality and contemplation. It is the largest mosque in the world, with minarets that reach almost to the sky. The interior dome is supported by pillars, each adorned with over gold-plated crescents.

The simple act of standing on a carpet in front of a large crowd and praying is called Salah. Salah, which means "prostration," is performed five times a day by Muslims as part of their religious prayer routine. There is one special prayer called Tahajud that is offered in the third part of the night.

Umrah is a pilgrimage to Mecca that Muslims make at least once in their lifetime if they can afford it. It's also an opportunity for Muslims around the world to get together and pray together with other Muslims who live in different countries. It's so cool when we all come together for Ramadan and Eid al-Fitr or Ramadan and Eid al-Adha. Umrah can be performed at any time of the year. The primary purpose of Umrah is to seek forgiveness for sins and seek blessings from Allah.

Umrah is one of the five pillars of Islam. Umrah is a ritual that can be performed by a person who enters the Sacred Mosque in Makkah. The ritual involves circumambulating the House (Kaabah) seven times and praying towards Qibla (facing Kaabah). It also includes several extra parts known as "Tawaf" (Circumambulation of Kaabah). Only a few lucky people get a chance to visit the House of Allah.

Unexpected Plan

Traveling to Umrah has been on my wish list for a long time. But I didn't do anything about it until recently. I wanted to spend some quality time in the worship (Ibadat) of Allah as my inner self had become quite difficult. I had no money to spend on Umrah (a short pilgrimage for Muslims), except for some savings. I was so depressed and thought that this was the end of me. Allah inserted a thought in my mind to perform Umrah. My journey was destined, so I never thought of money problems and whatever savings I had, I spent on my journey. In the past, I have performed Hajj and Umrah twice. This was my third visit to Saudi Arabia. My heart was yearning to see Kaabah after COVID. The moment I heard that Umrah tours are now operational, I immediately decided to plan my trip. I found it beneficial in all aspects of my life. It took me two weeks to plan everything properly, but I am glad that I did it because this year is the best year of my life. I called my Pakistani cousin and explained about my sudden plan to visit Makkah and Madinah. She was very happy with my decision. She expressed her interest in joining me on the Umrah Journey with her son. Out of joy, I immediately said this would be wonderful. And then my cousin and I were talking about our dream trip to Saudi Arabia and the conversation just spilled out. We were thinking of doing Umrah together and we wanted it to be an all-around memorable experience, which was not just religious but also outside the city!

We started picturing a trip to the Kingdom. For the same tours and travels, we have planned our accommodation and transportation. The only difference was that she was traveling from Pakistan and I am from India. My family members also felt happy with this decision and they all agreed that it is a smart idea for us to perform Umrah together. This will enable us to spend quality time together.

I started preparing for Umrah as soon as I decided that I would finally travel. I already had the application form ready and filled in, so my next step was to apply for leave. I got my leave application approved and started shopping for Umrah clothes and accessories.

The first thing I did was to buy some clothes for the journey. I chose two dresses, one of which was a black hijab. The other dress was a denim blue hijab. I also kept a few comfy regular dresses in my bag. Next, I bought a pair of shoes and socks for each day of the trip. Finally, I purchased all the essential accessories for the trip. Now that everything is ready, it's time to get started!

ﭖﭖﭖ

Umrah is a pilgrimage to Mecca that Muslims make at least once in their lifetime if they can afford it. It's also an opportunity for Muslims around the world to get together and pray together with other Muslims who live in different countries. It's so cool when we all come together for Ramadan and Eid al-Fitr or Ramadan and Eid al-Adha. Umrah can be performed at any time of the year. The primary purpose of Umrah is to seek forgiveness for sins and seek blessings from Allah.

Many people who make the Hajj don't opt for Umrah instead because the two pilgrimages are similar in many ways. It's not only one of the most picturesque trips in the world, but it's also one of the most spiritual. The most amazing thing is you get to travel between Mecca and Medina.

Umrah is one of the five pillars of Islam. Umrah is a ritual that can be performed by a person who enters the Sacred Mosque in Makkah. The ritual involves circumambulating the House (Kaabah) seven times and praying towards Qibla. It also includes several extra parts known as "Tawaf". Only a few lucky people get a chance to visit the House of Allah.

ﻣﻣﻣ

2
The Dreamy Flight

My mother was worried as I was traveling alone to Saudi Arabia, but she didn't want to say anything. I had convinced her that I would be fine. She knew that it was my decision and she would support me. My brother asked me if I wanted him to accompany me. He also wanted to know what kind of things I needed for my trip. However, I told him that he doesn't need to worry about anything as long as I am safe and sound.

My family planned to drop me off at the Bus Station, as my bus was scheduled to travel from Indore to Mumbai. We left home on time and reached there at around 9:30 PM. Fortunately our bus arrived on time. We started boarding the bus. It started at 10.00 PM. All Haajis were set to embark on their Umrah Journey. This was my solo trip to Saudi Arabia and I did it all alone.

I had a wonderful journey from Indore to Mumbai. It was a very comfortable journey with AC and other facilities. The driver was very friendly and helpful in every way.

In the morning, we arrived at Mumbai airport. It was a long big day. Our flight was scheduled for 9:00 PM. We were supposed to spend our day outside the airport for a few hours. After a full day of waiting, at 5.00 PM we were ready to check in and get the boarding pass. The process was very smooth; there were no delays or problems with the check-in. I took my time in the queue for the security check because it took a bit longer than usual due to some technical issues with the machine. I had to pass through a metal detector and then they took my phone and asked me about it. After the airport process, we performed Islamic Umrah rituals at Mumbai airport before boarding the plane. When we got on the plane, I thought about how much time had passed since my last visit in 2018.

I was flying from Mumbai to Jeddah, Saudi Arabia. The flight was about three hours long and the weather was very pleasant. I had a window seat which was suitable for capturing photos of the beautiful sky. I took lots of photos on my phone. Even though it was not possible to get them all on my phone, this is what I took away with me as a memory of my journey.

I had a great time taking pictures of the plane's wings. It was so cold in the cabin that my hands were frozen. But fortunately, there was some sort of heating system that kept things cozy and toasty. The seats were spacious and there were two in a row. The food was delicious and it was served on time. The flight attendants also gave us drinks after takeoff. This was helpful because we could drink during takeoff if we wanted or needed something stronger later on in our journey. The staff was helpful and friendly.

I sat down and looked around at all of the people around me. Some children and adults were trying to work on laptops or tablets. And then there were families with their babies who were sleeping in their laps or under blankets on the seat next to them. It's amazing how many people live on this planet and how many different ways there are for people to get by without technology!

I watched as one woman tried to take pictures of everything around her with her phone—but she missed some pretty amazing things as she took photos of her breakfast instead!

I was very happy to be on this flight. It was exciting for me; I wanted to see Kaabah after 4 long years. It was a long journey. I didn't even know when I fell asleep. And, I was only dreaming about Kaabah.

ᗪᗪᗪ

3
Soothing Makkah

I was in a deep sleep; the aunt next to me woke me up, saying we had finally reached Jeddah. How long have I waited for this day? I woke up with happiness. I am a Muslim girl who has been blessed to have embarked on the Umrah pilgrimage. I was glad that we arrived at Jeddah Airport. After all the security checks, we boarded a bus to travel from Jeddah to the Holy City of Makkah. When it finally arrived, we headed straight to our hotel to store our luggage in the hotel rooms. The first thing that struck me as soon as we stepped into our hotel in Makkah was the strong sense of spirituality and belonging.

On the other hand, I was very excited to meet my Pakistani cousin who was waiting for me in the hotel room along with her son. She reached Makkah one day before me, her Umrah was done. She was eagerly waiting for me, as I was reuniting with her after 4 years. I rushed to the room and met her. She greeted me with a hug and tears of joy. I was then dropped off at the hotel lounge.

My tour manager was waiting for us in the hotel lounge to accompany us to Masjid Al Harram. I was a bit smarter than most of the pilgrims, so my tour manager assigned me to support the females during their rituals. It was another blessing from Allah. I got a chance to earn more rewards by helping other naïve pilgrims. After that, I started my long-awaited ritual. I have shown my gratitude to Allah. I have finally reached Mecca with blessings from Allah. I have been fortunate enough to be able to learn a lot about Islam in these past months. I am fully convinced that this is the religion for me.

The Holy City Makkah is so alive with people coming from all over the world to perform this sacred ritual in peace and tranquility. The most meaningful lesson I learned is that Islam is not just about rituals but about a way of life. Pilgrimage is a time of spiritual, physical, and psychological growth as well as reflection, contemplation, and self-reflection. The second biggest lesson was the sheer diversity of the Muslim community; there were so many different people from so many different backgrounds performing this journey for many different reasons.

The ritual begins with entering the Ihram, which requires men to wear two white sheets (only for Men) and refrain from cutting their hair, nails, and shaving for the duration of Umrah. This is intended to exclude such activities as "abnormal sexual intercourse, alcohol drinking, and use of narcotics in any way" during the time they are in Mecca. It is a wise idea for pilgrims to brush up on their Arabic language skills before they go to Mecca. This is because it is not easy to get around without speaking Arabic. Dressing moderately is strongly recommended for women if they intend to perform Umrah while keeping in mind all the activities that are excluded.

With the blessings of Allah, we were able to complete our spiritual activities. Alhamdullilah (All praise to the Lord). It was a day full of contentment and happiness. In addition, I received compliments from other pilgrims for helping them with their rituals.

ᕘᕘᕘ

The Masjid Al Haram is the most sacred place on earth for Muslims. It is located in Makkah, Saudi Arabia. Muslims from across the world come to visit this holy place during the Umrah/Hajj period. When a person enters it, through the door of faith the heart becomes pure with love and submission to Allah. Upon entering a Masjid, the five senses are filled with beauty. The Kaabah, built by Abraham and Ismael is a magnificent structure. It represents the importance of human beings in the sight of Allah.

It is a mosque that was built over 1,000 years ago and is still in use today. The building is made of white marble, which gives it a very clean modern look. It has a huge courtyard that can fit thousands of people at once and a courtyard inside that has smaller rooms for praying. There are also many other buildings around the area for different purposes, such as schools and hospitals.

The mosque has become an iconic symbol for Islam and Muslims everywhere because it represents peace and harmony with its gorgeous architecture and peaceful surroundings. When you visit it, you will feel as though you've traveled back in time to an era when people were more religious than they are now; if only we could go back in time!

4
Glowing Message

It has been a few months since I embarked on my Umrah trip, but the memories are still fresh. It was a life-changing experience that left an everlasting impact on me. However, you can never really understand the significance of something until you experience it personally. The purpose of this chapter is to explain what I learned from this experience.

- **Be kind to others.**

Your hajj/umrah experience is meant to be shared with everyone. The people who are with you on this trip are also suffering through their struggles, and your kindness and compassion can make a huge difference in their lives. If someone needs help, offer your hand. If someone wants to talk, be there for them. Also, be extra kind to the people who serve you throughout your stay in Makkah and Madinah. This includes the shuttle bus driver, the hotel staff, and the gift shop employees. Remember, you have the opportunity to leave a positive impact on the lives of others, and you never know whose life you will change by being kind to them.

- **Remember why you're there.**

For many of us, this is a once-in-a-lifetime opportunity, so it's key to remember why you're there. Try to focus on your intention for embarking on the hajj/umrah. Ask yourself what you want to accomplish during this trip. This trip is for you to get closer to Allah, so don't forget why you came. Remember that you are now in Makkah Mukarramah, the most sacred place on Earth. You are in the presence of the most sacred house of worship on Earth. Reminding yourself of the significance of your surroundings will help you stay focused and on track with your intentions while on hajj/umrah.

- **Never stop praising Allah, even when you're at home.**

Remember to praise Allah as often as possible, even when you're at home. One of the most significant rituals in Islam is salah or prayer. Your daily prayers are the right way to make yourself mindful of Allah and His presence in your life. Your salah will also help keep you on track with your intention of traveling on the Hajj/umrah. Say plenty of dua (supplications to Allah), especially when you need something. Ask Allah for help and guidance, and let Him know that you are sincerely in need of something from Him. Don't ever think that Allah is not listening to you, or that your prayers are not being answered. Allah is always listening, and He always answers our dua.

- **Take care of your physical body.**

Your body is a gift that Allah has given you, so take care of it. Make sure to drink a lot of water, stay hydrated, and get plenty of rest. The heat of Saudi Arabia can sometimes be extremely intense, so make sure to stay cool and hydrated. Eating healthy will give you the energy you need to get the most out of this amazing trip. You also have to remember that you are fasting during this trip, so you should be careful to eat healthy while you are there. You are not just performing on hajj/umrah for yourself; you are also representing your loved ones, your community, and your country. You don't want to affect the health of your body and make yourself unable to continue the rituals or have your fellow pilgrims worrying about your health.

- **You are not alone; Allah is always with you.**

As soon as you land in Saudi Arabia, you will realize that you are not alone. You will be surrounded by the love of Allah, His Prophet, and his companions. You will feel that you are no longer alone and you will be surrounded by the blessings of Allah and His love. You will be able to feel the love of the Prophet and his companions. You will be given the opportunity to experience the love of the Ummah. You will be able to experience the love of Allah and you will be able to sense His love for you as well. This feeling is indescribable. You will realize that Allah loves you so much that He has sent you His Prophet and his companions to guide you to the righteous path. You will feel the love that Allah has for you. You will be able to feel the love that your Prophet and his companions have for you as well.

- **Always ask for help.**

No matter how strong you are and how much you try to rely on yourself, sometimes you just can't do it all on your own. You need to ask people around you for help, especially during your hajj/umrah journey. You can help others as well, but don't be afraid to look for help. Allah created us as a community, and we need to remember to rely on each other and offer each other support. There is nothing wrong with asking for help, or seeking assistance. There will be moments when you'll feel tired, or you'll just prefer to spend some time alone. There will be moments when you'll want to cry because of the overwhelming feeling of gratitude and love you'll feel. There will be moments when you'll realize that you are so grateful for this experience, and you don't expect anything to disrupt it. There will be moments when you'll be completely overwhelmed, and you'll just want someone to quietly sit with you and hold your hand.

- **The days after your tawaf.**

Your hajj/umrah journey doesn't end with your tawaf. It's the beginning of a new journey that you have the opportunity to shape however you want. Keep your intention of performing hajj/umrah in mind after you finish your tawaf. Remind yourself of the things you want to accomplish during this trip. It's easy to get caught up in the excitement of the moment and forget your intentions, so keep a point to stay focused and grounded. You've made it to Makkah, and now you're ready to embark on a journey of a lifetime. These are the days that you'll never forget, so make them count. It doesn't matter how old you are or when you set out on your first Umrah trip; everyone's experience is different. You will most likely walk away with the most memorable memories of your life. You will become a different person after the experience, and you will never be the same again. Now that you know what to expect and how to prepare for your Umrah trip, you can't wait to book your flights and turn this trip into a reality. Remember, it's not just a trip; it's a journey toward self-growth and spiritual enlightenment. It's time to follow in the footsteps of Prophet Muhammad, Sallallahu 'Alayhi wa Sallam. I hope this trip will be one of the most memorable parts of your life.

5
Force of Gravity

"Distance means so little when someone means so much."

I can't believe it's been five years since we last saw each other. I can't believe that time has flown by so quickly, but it has. I thought about him all day and couldn't get my mind off of him.

In Makkah, I reunited with my personal favorite Zaroon after five years. It was not a normal meeting. It was not decided whether we would meet in Makkah. As Zaroon was busy with his job responsibilities, he told me earlier that maybe we would not meet this time in Saudi Arabia due to an unexpected situation.

Let me tell you the story from the beginning. The decision to leave Makkah on Thursday was made by our tour manager, and I informed Zaroon that we were leaving Makkah on Thursday. Suddenly in the evening, our manager said, "I think, we should spend one more Friday in Makkah, as we will have more time for Ibadat." My cousin and I were very happy that we would spend one more day in Makkah. We decided to offer Tahajjud prayer (a special prayer in the third part of the night) in Masjid Al Harram. We walked from our hotel room to the Masjid. Then, we

"

offered Tahajjud and Fajr (morning prayer) in the Masjid. While sitting in the mosque after Namaz, I hear the beep of my mobile. It was Zaroon's msg. He asked me, "Reached Madinah?". Out of joy, I replied, "No, we are spending our Friday in Makkah today, in the afternoon we have a bus for Madinah". He sent an emoticon and asked, "Do you believe in surprises?" I said, "Yes, I do". "Your day is going to be filled with a wonderful surprise", he said. Perplexed, I thought I would surely receive a reward from Allah since I was in Makkah.

After reading his message, I headed to the hotel to have breakfast and get ready for Friday. I had a bath, dressed up in a beautiful hijab. I was supposed to accompany my sister, but due to her body pain, she suggested I go to the mosque to offer tawaaf (Circumambulation of Kaabah) and salah. I walked alone from my hotel to the mosque. Alhamdulillah, I entered the mosque again, and I offered two tawaaf that day. Zohar Namaz (afternoon prayer) was soon approaching. I found the female area and sat there to read Surah Kahf (a chapter from the Quran). I completed Surah, and then checked my mobile to see where my sister is. Having limited internet data on my mobile, I switched on the internet and found Zaroon's message saying, "Where are you? Call me right after Friday prayers." I responded, "Certainly." I was thinking perhaps it was his holiday so he wants to talk to me. I had no idea what was going on at his side.

After Friday prayers, I called him. "Meet at Gate No. 89", he told me. I asked, "Are you kidding?", and he replied, "No, seriously I'm here." I asked, "Is it a surprise or a heart attack?" I was shivering knowing that he was in the masjid, it was like a dream come true after 5 years. I was like what is happening to me? I was surprised because all I had asked

Allah at that time was that I wanted to see Zaroon in Ehraam in Masjid al Harram. It was a beautiful dua, accepted at a beautiful time. Zaroon answered the call and said he would be there to meet me. It felt like my most beautiful prayer. Ufffff...

I was navigating through so many emotions at the same time. After all, I was meeting him after 5 years. It was like a dream come true at just the right time. I have missed him so much over these years. I came outside and started calling him. He was offering two rakats (two units of prayer) in front of Makaam-e-Ibraahim. He prayed and then walked outside.

We met at Gate No.89 outside Masjid Al Harram. We were both in a rush to get there and got lost a few times but we finally made it. Then we talked briefly near WC 3. We felt like this was the most appropriate moment to meet.

Only Allah knows what he has in store for us. If Allah wants everything happens. We met only because of Allah. It was truly a miracle that I was able to see Zaroon in Ehraam on the same day I wanted to see him.

So finally, I met Mr. Perfect.

Me: I am very happy to see you after 5 years

Z: Even I felt happy.

Me: Zaroon, we have very limited time. My bus is scheduled to leave at 2.00 PM for Madinah. Could you please drop me at my hotel? We can spend some time with each other while walking.

He wanted to take me for lunch, but due to limited time, we couldn't. He agreed to drop me off at the hotel. On the way to the hotel, we had a pleasant conversation. That day was very difficult for me. My luggage was kept in my room on the 13th floor. There was a hustle and bustle. The time was shrinking. My cousin called me and said, "Please go to the hotel restaurant and eat something". Then she arranged my luggage on the bus.

Zaroon and I walked to a restaurant to have lunch. It was destiny that there was only one lunch plate, and without any thought, I put it on the table and told Zaroon to eat from it. We both ate from the same lunch plate. It was not a romantic date. However, if you think about it peacefully, you will analyze that meetings arranged by Allah are way more beautiful than meetings arranged by us. We had tea and walked downstairs as there was a rush near the lift. The tour manager told us to head towards the bus as it was now late as we reached the lounge area.

Zaroon and I wanted to talk but we couldn't due to limited time. He told me not to worry and said he would join me in Madinah. He assured me that he would meet me and encouraged me to relax. He dropped me off at the bus and said not to worry. He was also worried about my lunch as I did not eat properly. Zaroon is a shining example of a gentleman. He understands before I say anything. I was happy to meet him but disappointed about the limited time we had.

My eyes were constantly fixed on the rear view mirror of the bus, trying to catch a glimpse of Zaroon. There's something about Zaroon that makes me feel so connected. My life revolves around him. This life is too short to love him. It was a brief but amazing time together and I felt blessed that I met him!

Leaving Makkah behind, our bus bid farewell. It was a sad day, but we were also happy because we were en route to Madinah "City of Prophet Muhammad PBUH".

6
Peaceful Madinah

Beauty of Madinah

It's nearly impossible to find the words to describe the beauty of Madinah. It's a city of peace, where people are free to practice religion at its highest level and live their lives as they please. It's a place where you can find ancient walls, mosques, and gardens that have stood for centuries. It's a place that has been home to some of the most powerful and influential people in history—from Prophet Muhammad (peace be upon him) and Companions to kings and queens—and it will always welcome us with open arms. If you're ever in the area, don't miss the beauty of Madinah!

Madinah is known as a place of pilgrimage for Muslims, and it is where Muhammad (PBUH) made his final retreat before his death.

The city is home to many mosques, including the Prophet's Mosque (Masjid Nabawi) and Masjid-e-Quba which is considered to be one of the most significant mosques in Islam.

I have been to Madinah three times, and every time I return, it feels like a brand-new experience. The city is so full of history and culture that it feels like it has hardly changed at all over the centuries. But as you walk through its streets, you can see how much has changed since Muhammad lived there.

The first thing that strikes me about Madinah is its beauty. Even after all these years, it still feels like a place where you could see angels or even prophets walking along the streets. I love visiting Madinah's markets because they are always bustling with activity from people buying fresh produce from local farmers and selling their crafts. These markets also attract visitors from around the world who come to shop for special items for their homes or businesses back home. When I am in Madinah, I always find myself wandering through one of its many souks looking for something interesting to buy for myself.

ppp

Masjid-Al-Harram

It was a beautiful day in Madinah Munawwarah, and we were all excited to visit Masjid-Al-Haram in Madinah Munawwarah. We arrived at the mosque and walked toward the prayer area. We offered our prayers and praised Almighty Allah for the opportunity given. It was such a memorable day.

Imagine the feeling of being part of something bigger than yourself.

You're part of a community, and you're part of a religion. You're part of a family—a family that's wider than just your friends and their families, but also a family that's much larger than any other family in the world.
And you're able to make time for something so significant to you every single day. Every day, without fail, without fail!

I was blessed with the opportunity to take part in an amazing community gathering at Masjid-Al-Haram Madinah.

The Masjid, which is located in the heart of Madinah, is one of the most striking mosques I've ever seen. The interior design is truly breathtaking and makes you feel like you're walking through a museum or a living history museum. The entire area surrounding the mosque is a park where people come to relax and enjoy the peaceful atmosphere.

It is the policy of the authorities to provide opportunities for prayer to every single individual who enters the mosque area. It's their way of giving back to their community and encouraging people from all walks of life to come together for prayer, study, and socializing. Their goal is simple: they want to help people connect with Allah through prayer as well as educate them about Islam in general so they can become better Muslims (or at least better-educated ones!).

I had an incredible time at this gathering! I got so much out of it—not only did I learn more about Islam (what it's about), but also how much fun it can be when people come together to pray!

ᐁᐁᐁ

Riyazul Jannah

The area between the Minbar and the sacred chamber of Prophet Muhammad PBUH in Masjid Al Nabawi is called Riyazul Jannah. It is one of the gardens of Paradise. Prophet Muhammad PBUH said, "One salat (prayer) is better than one thousand prayers in any other Masjid, except for Masjid Al Harram.

The experience of offering prayer at Riyazul Jannah is a truly beautiful and spiritual one. The atmosphere is calm and quiet. With every step you take, you feel as if you are entering into a new world where everything is possible, where there is nothing to fear.

You can feel the presence of Allah (SWT) in your heart as you offer your prayer. You will be surprised at how easy it is to connect with Him through this beautiful place.

You feel like you can do anything, and that nothing can ever bring you down. You know that God is always there for you, no matter what happens—and that He loves each and every one of His creations with an unconditional love that is so powerful it cannot be measured.

Offering prayer at Riyazul Jannah is also about the way it makes you think about yourself and your life. When we pray for things, we're actually asking Allah SWT to help us solve our problems! We're asking Him to help us get what we want out of life—and it works! It works so well that sometimes we forget just how amazing our lives are—how blessed we are—and spend more time worrying about things than enjoying them. This is why offering prayer at this place allows us to see ourselves as Allah SWT sees us: beautiful creatures made by Him in His image and deserving of His love and protection.

Everyone who visits this land feels happy because they have been blessed by Allah (SWT) himself with such an amazing gift!

I pray to Allah that He blesses you with the best of all worlds. May He grant you all the goodness, love, and happiness in this world and beyond. Summa Ameen.

ᐅᐅᐅ

Dar Al Madinah Museum

The first and largest museum that specializes in the history of Almadinah and its deep heritage. The museum highlights the history of the city of our beloved prophet, peace be upon him, as well as its valuable heritage and rich ancient civilization. The museum displays a substantial collection of hand-built models that show you a simulation of the actual old landmarks of the city as well as a substantial collection of rear pieces and rear shoots of the city and its history.

My cousin and I decided to visit the Madinah Museum on the next day of our trip to Madinah. It is situated near Masjid Al Nabawi. The museum is air-conditioned. We bought our tickets on-site and requested an Urdu-speaking guide. The guide was informative, spoke clearly, and answered all our questions patiently.

THIS PLACE IS AMAZING! You must not miss this museum. My tour group did not bring me to this place so we decided (me and my cousin) to visit it on our own. I felt incredibly sorry for the rest of my group because they didn't get to experience this. I sat for days in Masjid Nabawi trying to imagine what it was like during the Prophet's time, and this place satisfied my curiosity. They explained everything about Madinah and Makkah during the time of the prophet through dioramas and artifacts. Something about seeing the story visually and seeing what the prophet's house looked like and how it progressed to Masjid Nabawi helped me appreciate my Madinah experience more. I felt like I was reliving the past. The tour guide spoke in Urdu, was very knowledgeable and helpful and he explained the stories so well. I learned so much about the Prophet's Seerah and I'm so grateful for the experience.

We learned quite a bit. We also got a chance to watch 3D movies from ancient times for free. At the end of the tour, we were offered dates and tea. The staff were all so friendly. When I was sitting alone in the waiting room, one of the staff offered me Arabic coffee and I thought that was a lovely gesture. Must visit.

ᗐᗐᗐ

Madinah Market

The first and largest museum that specializes in the history of Almadinah and its deep heritage. The museum highlights the history of the city of our beloved prophet, peace be upon him, as well as its valuable heritage and rich ancient civilization. The museum displays a substantial collection of hand-built models that show you a simulation of the actual old landmarks of the city as well as a substantial collection of rear pieces and rear shoots of the city and its history.

My cousin and I decided to visit the Madinah Museum on the next day of our trip to Madinah. It is situated near Masjid Al Nabawi. The museum is air-conditioned. We bought our tickets on-site and requested an Urdu-speaking guide. The guide was informative, spoke clearly, and answered all our questions patiently.

THIS PLACE IS AMAZING! You must not miss this museum. My tour group did not bring me to this place so we decided (me and my cousin) to visit it on our own. I felt incredibly sorry for the rest of my group because they didn't get to experience this. I sat for days in Masjid Nabawi trying to imagine what it was like during the Prophet's time, and this place satisfied my curiosity. They explained everything about Madinah and Makkah during the time of the prophet through dioramas and artifacts. Something about seeing the story visually and seeing what the prophet's house looked like and how it progressed to Masjid Nabawi helped me appreciate my Madinah experience more. I felt like I was reliving the past. The tour guide spoke in Urdu, was very knowledgeable and helpful and he explained the stories so well. I learned so much about the Prophet's Seerah and I'm so grateful for the experience.

We learned quite a bit. We also got a chance to watch 3D movies from ancient times for free. At the end of the tour, we were offered dates and tea. The staff were all so friendly. When I was sitting alone in the waiting room, one of the staff offered me Arabic coffee and I thought that was a lovely gesture. Must visit.

ᗞᗞᗞ

Special Daawat at Mataam Mehran

Our daawat at Mataam Mehran Restaurant in Madinah with our tour manager was an experience to remember. Our Daawat was not given to anyone else but us. We supported our tour manager during the entire journey, and we helped all Haajis. He was happy with my cousin and my support. Out of courtesy, he offered us Daawat at one of the finest restaurants in Madinah.

We drove to Mataam Mehran. The experience was so yummy. The biryani was so delicious that we didn't want it to end. We had to keep on eating it! The chicken was roasted to perfection and tasted heavenly. Our tour manager even made sure that we didn't have any leftovers.

In addition to the biryani and roasted chicken, we also had a wide variety of other dishes including mutton kebabs and chicken curry. All of the food at Mataam Mehran Restaurant was amazing, but the biryani stood out as the most delicious part of our daawat because it was so rich with flavor and spices.

ﭖﭖﭖ

7

Unforgettable Visit to Saudi Family

I had the pleasure of visiting a Saudi family for the first time on this Umraah trip. I was blown away by the warm welcome I received from my cousin's friend.

My cousin worked at King Faisal Hospital for four years. She made so many friends of different nationalities. The moment we entered Madinah, she informed all of her friends about our stay near Masjid-Al-Harram, Madinah. A friend of hers invited us to her beautiful home. As this was my first visit to an Arab family, I was looking forward to interacting with them. It was a pleasure to visit her house. I enjoyed receiving such a warm welcome from a Saudi friend.

My visit to Saudi Family was a memorable experience. I felt welcomed and cared for by the Saudi friend, who made us feel at home during our stay. She provided us with a warm and friendly environment. She prepared yummier meals for us. We enjoyed the fantastic variety of dishes. She even let us try some of their delicious food!

She also asked if I needed anything and then showed me around the house. I was mesmerized by the beauty of the home. She led us into the kitchen and showed us where everything was kept. There were many spices and foods that I had never seen before. She made sure to explain all of them to me as she cooked them. Then she invited us to sit down at the table while she talked about life in Saudi Arabia.

I must say that she lives in one of the most peaceful places you can imagine. This makes it easy for them to enjoy life with their families without having to worry about anything else.

I had been to the country many times before, but never like this. The experience gave me the opportunity to see everything from a fresh perspective. It was incredible to see how much they loved their home country and what it meant to them.

We spent the rest of the time talking about our own cultures: hers being Lebanese and mine being Indian. We got along so well!

Lebanese by birth and Arab by marriage, she is married to an Arab. Nursing was her profession. The first time her husband saw her was during one of the training sessions in the hospital. He then proposed marriage to her. She told us that her husband had been working for several years as a trainer before they got married. I asked her how long they'd been married, and she told me that it was only two years ago, making us feel even more welcome during this trip! We sat down and chatted for hours over coffee and sweets, talking about how they met and how they got hitched.

It was an unforgettable experience that I will never forget.

8
The Last Day

We were scheduled to depart from Jeddah Airport on May 27, 2022. We left Madinah in the afternoon by bus. It was an extremely difficult day as I was leaving Madinah "The City of the Prophet". On the same day, my cousin was also traveling to her home country. Goodbyes are so difficult. I wasn't in tune, I was sobbing. My sister consoled me and said I should walk to the mosque to offer my Zuhr (afternoon) prayers. She said, don't stay with me otherwise you will have a hard time saying goodbye to me. I walked to the Masjid, and again I was in tears because I had seen Roza-e-Rasool. I wasn't sure when I would come back here again. With the promise of returning to Madinah again, I prayed a lot in Harram (inside the Mosque). By the time I arrived at the hotel to board a bus to Jeddah, my sister had already been to the airport to catch her flight. It was a hard day for us.

We boarded the bus. We began our journey from Madinah to Jeddah. It was a six-hour trip. I intentionally left the seat next to me blank. My reservation was for Zaroon since he had promised to meet me in Madinah and accompany me from Madinah to Jeddah. It is different that he did not show up. To feel his presence, I kept a blank seat next to me. I didn't want anyone to sit near me. I wanted to discuss many things with him about the future. But destiny had something else for us. He has confirmed that he will be at Jeddah Airport to welcome me when I arrive. I was so excited to see him in person! All week, he had been calling and messaging me, and I had been yearning to meet him. If you remember, we met in Makkah on Friday for a few minutes and he dropped me off at my bus to Madinah.

At 7.30 PM, our bus reached the Jeddah airport. Our Umrah group had to sit in the airport waiting area. It was Hajj Terminal, Gate No. 3. Everyone except me was waiting to check in; I was experiencing anxiety attacks as Zaroon hadn't yet arrived. It was 8.30 PM. It was time for us to get inside the airport. We picked up our luggage, shifted it to the trolley, and headed towards the main gate of the Hajj Terminal. My heartbeats were high, my mind was blank, and my feet were immobile. There was sweat streaming down my forehead, and I was unable to think clearly. Zaroon was the only thing on my mind. Where is he? I was constantly wondering. My flight time was 11.00 PM. Our flight was only 90 minutes away. It was challenging to coordinate everything, like checking in, boarding, security check, and meeting Zaroon, in these few minutes. Every second was making me more anxious.

He was constantly on the phone with me. He was on his way. There were so many gifts I brought for him. In my heart, I wanted to present it to him. I had a heavy handbag as a result of those gifts. Many thoughts were running through my head, such as what would happen if I didn't meet him.

I arranged a Biryani pack for him that evening since I wanted to have dinner with him. I didn't eat anything, as I kept thinking I would eat with him. It is rare for us to spend quality time together. Since I was meeting him after five years, I did not want to miss a single opportunity to spend time with him.

The phone started ringing. Zaroon was calling. He contacted me and said it was difficult to get in. He was not allowed to enter Hajj Terminal by airport authorities. He was asked to show his travel documents and when he couldn't produce them, they didn't allow him in. This was a challenge for Zaroon because he didn't know what to do. He attempted to reach the Hajj Terminal four times over an hour, but he was denied each time. He tried as hard as he could to enter. The airport police and Zaroon had a heated conversation. An argument broke out between Zaroon and the police at the airport. It even came to the point that the police threatened to revoke his license if he continued to annoy them. By giving the police so many reasons to allow him inside, Zaroon performed a hit-and-run. However, every trial failed.

He called me and said, "Maybe we won't meet this time, officers don't allow me". The tone of his voice was low and sorrowful. It was also quite disheartening for me. To see if something could work out, I talked to him and looked around. Immediately, I noticed taxis entering Hajj terminal 4. I recommended Zaroon take a taxi to enter. We were fortunate that it worked out. Ultimately, he reached the destination via taxi on his fifth attempt. I felt terrible that he had to suffer through all that just to meet me. I'm so grateful that he was able to persevere and make it to our meeting.

The meeting was challenging. He immediately called me and said, "Come outside, I'm here". I walked out to the gate and noticed him. We were getting a bit excited to see each other because we had been messaging and calling each other all this time. I was so happy to see him when he arrived at Jeddah Airport. Additionally, I noticed that he was holding a large bag. The bag was a gift for me. He brought me a gift packet filled with chocolates and dry fruits.

We stood near the barricades. On one side, I was facing him, and on the other side, he was facing me. It was seriously not a normal meeting. It was a scene straight out of a movie. There was a feeling of being on a border. We were separated by barricades as though someone tried to meet a criminal in jail. We couldn't do anything else but stand there and talk to each other. It was a short meeting; we started talking about the future. His face clearly showed that he was tired. I was so happy that Zaroon came to meet me. Zaroon was late. Throughout his day, he spent the majority of time checking that he hadn't forgotten anything. There was one thing he forgot: time management. Boys are terrible at managing their time. It is not only about him, but about every single man who has ever lived on this earth. His schedule was packed. There was no doubt that he was busy. But I believe a person should know how to set priorities. The most exciting part was that we were able to meet at last. I'm so glad that we were able to meet before I left for Saudi Arabia! Luckily everything worked out in the end.

Zaroon: The airport authorities made it difficult for me.

Me: I'm so glad you could make it to Jeddah Airport today! I was apprehensive that you wouldn't be able to get into Terminal 4, however, Allah helped us through.

Zaroon: I try my best to make everything alright, but it ends up being the opposite. I am so sorry.

Me: I know you're suffering a lot right now and I just want you to know how much I've missed you. Thank you again for coming all this way today—it means a lot to me that we could meet like this again!

Zaroon: You have changed a lot.

Me: Positive or Negative Change?

Zaroon: Amazingly positive.

(I smiled)

Zaroon: Did you eat your dinner?

Me: I wanted to have it with you. I have arranged a Biryani pack for you.

Zaroon: We don't have time to eat dinner. You eat your dinner on the plane. I think we must focus on talking.

Me: Yes. You are right.

Zaroon: I have gifts for you.

Me: Zaroon, I also have gifts for you.

Zaroon gave me all the gifts he brought for me. I also gave him gifts I brought for him. He was happy to see gifts, including that beautiful ring. Zaroon asked me out of surprise "Ring?". I said, "Yes, ring". I told him I wanted to put this ring on his finger. Zaroon Said, "I would like you to put this ring on my finger on special occasions in the future. Don't settle for less." We both smiled and had a wonderful conversation full of emotions. He is a very polite person and we had a pleasant talk.

He had come all the way to meet me and I was so happy to finally see him. We held each other's hands tightly. It was a pleasure to catch up with him and I'm so glad he came to visit me. We were approaching the memorable moments, but then the phone started ringing. My tour manager was calling me, as he was worried about my check-in process. He called me and said to come immediately, our flight time was approaching. Zaroon told me not to worry about anything. He said he was planning to come to India to meet me.

He told me to go straight to the main gate. He said, "I'm here to see you. I won't move until you're inside the airport". As I was walking, I kept turning to look at him again and again. It was as if I didn't want to leave him behind. I wanted to stand there with him, but it was not possible. I was crying. Zaroon called me and said, "Don't cry, I will be on call until you sit on the airplane".

He was on a call with me. I entered the airport, passed the security check, and boarded the airplane. I felt his virtual presence throughout the call. Bye is the hardest part. I did not want to cut the call, so I told Zaroon to stay on the call with me until it disconnected itself. Once the plane took off, there was no network, and the call dropped on its own. The moment that phone stopped working, I took a deep breath and prayed for the best for him. Allah's mercy will surely bring us back together on this special occasion of our lives. Aameen.

I know that this is the beginning of an incredible adventure for us both—and I am ready for whatever comes next! Well, I'm sure glad that I've got someone in my life who can be so honest with me about what's going on! He is an amazing part of my life.

I love the way he looks at me like I'm the most beautiful girl on earth and he can't imagine ever wanting anyone else. I love the way he makes me feel like we're the only two people in the world. I feel like there's no one else who matters as much as he and me.

And I know this is true because I've seen him struggle, and I've witnessed him get angry. In addition, I've seen him work hard to be the most effective version of himself for me. And it's not just about what he does for me—it's about what he does for other people too! The way he talks about his friends and gives them advice is amazing—he cares so much about other people that it shows up in everything that he does.

He makes me laugh, he makes me cry, and he makes me feel like there is nothing better than him in this world. And I know that sounds crazy—but it's true! I'm so glad that he came into my life and changed everything for the better.

During this journey, I learned about love, sacrifice, patience, trust, and the power of God.

The Almighty

The beauty of Almighty Allah is beyond compare. He is the most beautiful and loving of all.

He is the creator of all beings and all that exists. He has no form at all, yet still possesses beauty because of His love for us and our love for Him. He is Almighty and powerful, yet merciful to us. He loves us unconditionally and has given us a beautiful life on earth to live in peace with each other.

The prayer "Allahu Akbar" (God is Most Merciful) is a reminder that we are not alone; that there is Someone who loves us more than we could ever love ourselves. It reminds us that we have a purpose in this life: To worship God with our whole hearts, souls, and minds. That's why I say every morning when I wake up and every night when I retire to sleep: "God is the Greatest."

♡♡♡

Dear Allah,

Thank you for the beauty of your creation, and the peace that you have given us. Please help us to live a life of peace and tranquility, and help us to create beauty in our lives. Allow us to be more grateful for the gifts you have given us. Thank you for the love that you have bestowed upon us.

♡♡♡